PIANO • VOCAL • GUITAR

TOP COUNTRY HITS OF 2013-2014

ISBN 978-1-4803-8239-8

HAL•LEONARD® CORPORATION
7777 W. BLUEMOUND RD. P.O. BOX 13819 MILWAUKEE, WI 53213

Visit Hal Leonard Online at
www.halleonard.com

CAROLINA

Words and Music by RICK BEATO,
BARRY KNOX, JOSHUA McSQAIN,
MATT THOMAS and SCOTT THOMAS

CRUISE

Words and Music by CHASE RICE,
TYLER HUBBARD, BRIAN KELLEY,
JOEY MOI and JESSE RICE

Moderately fast

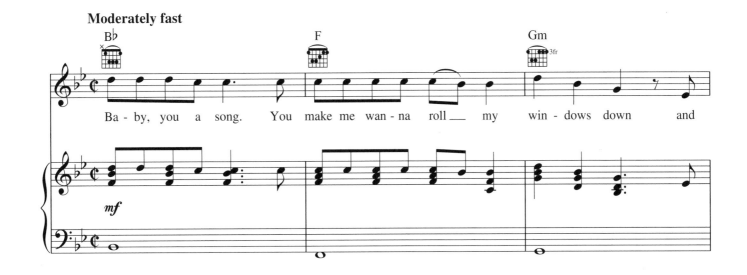

Ba - by, you a song. You make me wan - na roll __ my win - dows down and

cruise. __

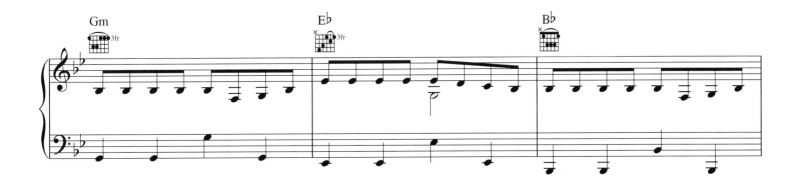

DRINK A BEER

Words and Music by JIM BEAVERS
and CHRIS STAPLETON

and drink a beer.

So long, _____ my friend, _

DRUNK LAST NIGHT

Words and Music by LAURA VELTZ
and JOSH OSBORNE

Moderately

I got a lit-tle drunk last night. _____

There's some-thin' 'bout a mid-night rain. _____

MINE WOULD BE YOU

Words and Music by CONNIE HARRINGTON,
DERIC RUTTAN and JESSICA ALEXANDER

THE OUTSIDERS

Words and Music by ERIC CHURCH
and CASEY BEATHARD

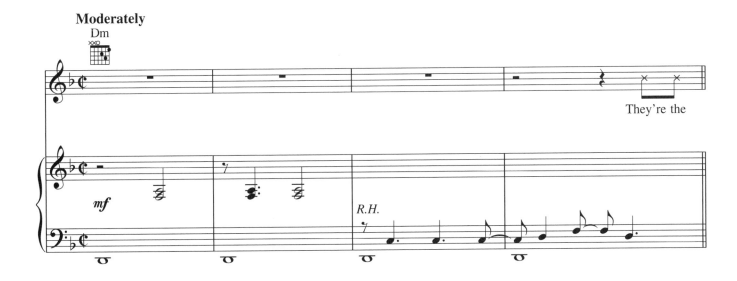

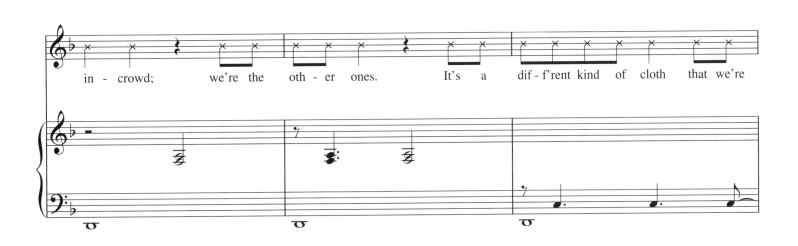

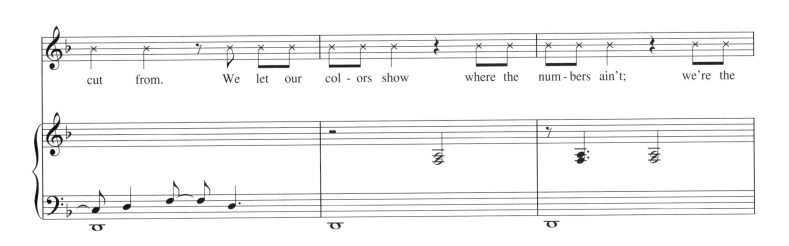

whoa, _____ the out - sid - ers.
(Whoa, _____ whoa.) ___

Fast

Rock Shuffle

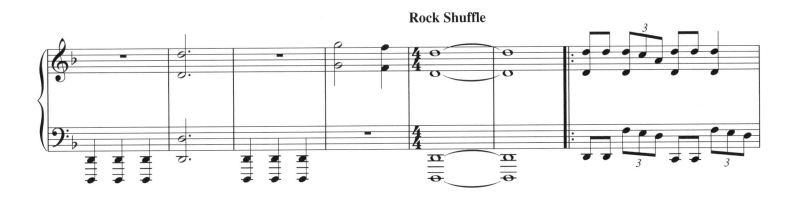

Freely

That's   who   we   are.

SOUTHERN GIRL

Words and Music by JAREN JOHNSTON,
LEE THOMAS MILLER and RODNEY CLAWSON

Moderately

STAY

Words and Music by JOHN YOUNG,
CHRISTOPHER ROBERTSON, JONATHAN LAWHON,
BEN WELLS and JOEY MOI

Recorded a half step higher.

SUNNY AND 75

Words and Music by JASON SELLERS,
PAUL JENKINS and MICHAEL DULANEY

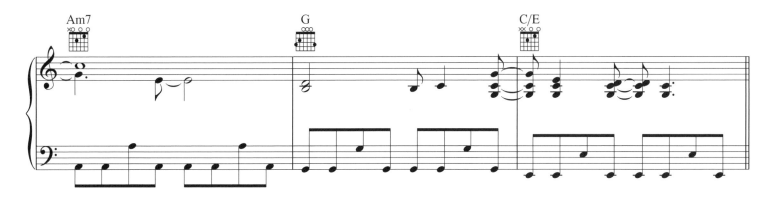

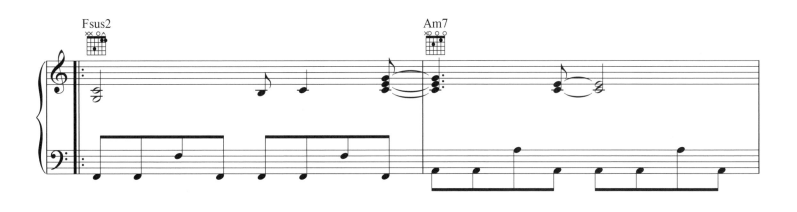

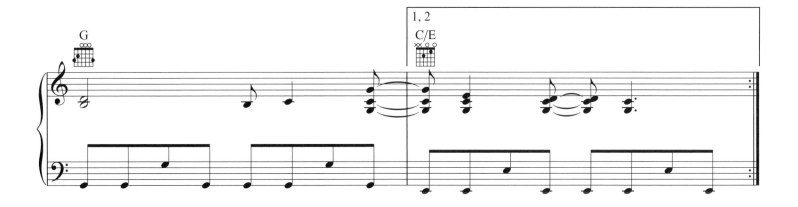

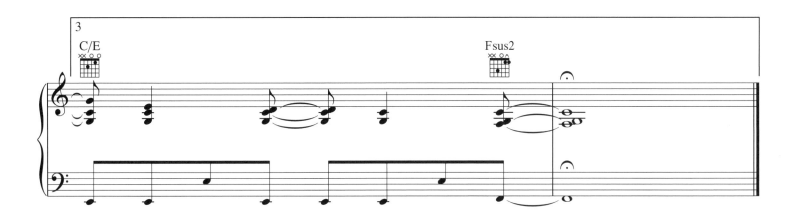

SURE BE COOL IF YOU DID

Words and Music by CHRIS TOMPKINS,
JIMMY ROBBINS and RODNEY CLAWSON

Recorded a half step lower.

SWEET ANNIE

Words and Music by ZAC BROWN,
WYATT DURRETTE, SONIA LEIGH
and JOHN PIERCE

*Recorded a half step higher.

THAT'S MY KIND OF NIGHT

Words and Music by DALLAS DAVIDSON,
CHRIS DESTEFANO and ASHLEY GORLEY

Moderately fast

I got that real good, feel good stuff up un-der the seat __ of my
dia-mond-plate tail-gate. Put in my _____ coun-try

big black jacked-up truck. Roll-in' on thir-ty-fives, _____ pret-ty girl by my
ride hip-hop mix tape: lit-tle Con-way, a lit-tle T-Pain. __ Might __ just make it

side. __ You got __ that sun-tan, skirt and boots. Wait-in' on you to
rain. __ You can hang your t-shirt on a limb. Hit __ that bank and

WASTING ALL THESE TEARS

Words and Music by CAITLYN SMITH
and ROLLIE GAALSWYK

tried to find ___ you at the bot - tom of a bot - tle, ___

lay - in' down ___ on the bath - room ___ floor. ___ My

WHATEVER SHE'S GOT

Words and Music by JIMMY ROBBINS
and JON NITE

Recorded a half step higher.

To Coda

100

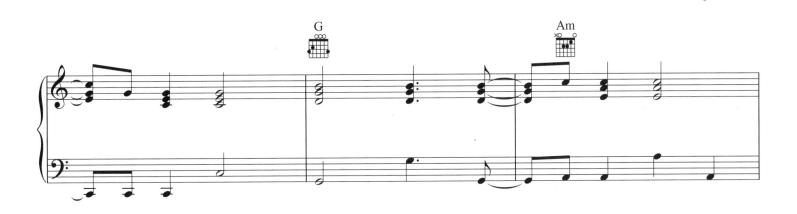

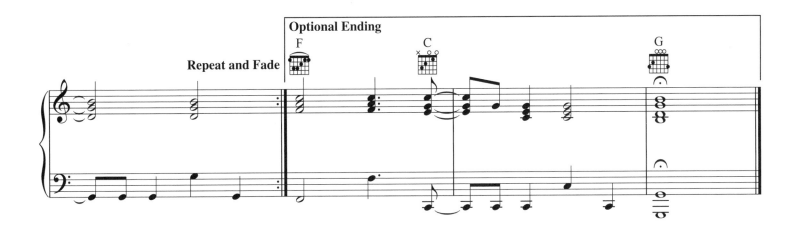

WE WERE US

Words and Music by JON NITE,
JIMMY ROBBINS and NICHOLLE GALYON